# Morning
## Tea *with* THE KING

*Daily Devotional*

## TISH BARNHARDT

# Become an author today!

## www.soarbookpublishing.com

**All scriptures are taken from the Kings James Version; King James Version, public domain.**

https://ioraprimarycare.com/blog/herbal-teabenefits/
https://www.developgoodhabits.com/herbaltea/?nonitro=1
https://simplelooseleaf.com/blog/herbal-tea/herbaltea-list-benefits

**Published by:** Soar Book Publishing

# Acknowledgements

I want to thank Tia Monique Randle for supporting me the whole way with getting my first personal book written. I appreciate your wisdom, your knowledge, and I am honored to have worked with you on this project. If anyone reading this book has a desire to write and you don't know where to start, please reach out to Tia Monique with Let It Out Academy for writing classes and to get you on your way to becoming a Best-Selling Author.

I also want to thank my three boys Jeremiah, Daniel, and Joshua Vaughn for being incredibly supportive of pushing their mom to write. I thank them openly for their prayers and words of encouragement.

## About the Author

Prophetess Latissua Barnhardt is a preacher, teacher, author, and lover of God's word. She believes in applying biblical principles to any and every situation in her life. She is the mother of three handsome young men, Jeremiah, Daniel, and Joshua Vaughn.

Stay updated on her new releases and upcoming events on her website at:

**www.tdbincorp.com and on Facebook at**

**https://www.facebook.com/Prophetesslatissua.vaughn**

# List of Herbal Teas & Benefits

**Chamomile Tea** - May help reduce inflammation, treat stomach pain, aid sleep, and promote calmness and muscle relaxation.

**Peppermint Tea** - May be used for its refreshing and calming properties. Tea has a lightly sweet and refreshing flavor that may help with bad breath. The most important benefits include stress relief, aiding digestion and soothing the stomach, boosting the immune system, and relieving the symptoms of common cold.

**Rosehip Tea** - May be a great source of vitamin C and antioxidants. It may help with achieving weight loss goals, and protect the brain and skin from aging.

**Rooibos Tea** - May be used not only for its flavor, but for its potent antioxidant activity and many potential benefits – from reducing cholesterol and high blood pressure to treating colic in infants and increasing airflow to the lungs.

**Ginger Tea** - May help with upset stomach and nausea. Ginger may have many more potential benefits–from protecting the brain and heart to lowering blood sugar and having anti-cancer properties.

**Cinnamon Tea** - May have antioxidant and anti-inflammatory properties and may help with lowering blood pressure and protecting the heart.

**Lemongrass Tea** - May help relieve pain and anxiety, lower blood pressure, may act as antioxidant, and may help with weight management. May also have antibacterial and anti-inflammatory properties.

**Olive Leaf Tea** - May have potential use in preventing cancer, lowering cholesterol and blood sugar, and helping with weight loss.

**Eucalyptus Tea** - May be known for its antiseptic and antibacterial properties, and may be helpful for different breathing and lung-related problems–from treating the common cold and flu to sore throat and pneumonia.

**Ashwagandha Tea** - May help with treating stress, anxiety and sleeping problems. May help protect the brain and heart, improve memory, and may even improve muscle strength.

**Raspberry Leaf Tea** - May be mostly used by pregnant women to shorten labor. Although drinking this tea may be considered safe in most cases, more research is needed to see if it can help and how safe it is.

**Elderberry Flower Tea** - May have antibacterial and antiviral properties. The flavonoids in elderberry flowers and berries may help in treating influenza, bronchitis, and pain relief.

**Moringa Tea** - May be helpful with heart diseases, diabetes, cancer, and fatty liver.

**Lavender Tea** - May be helpful for relaxation, relieving anxiety, calming, and lifting mood.

**Echinacea Tea** - May be helpful to use for the common cold and for treating depression.

**Jasmine Tea** - May be helpful in treating anxiety, fever, sunburn, and stomach ulcers.

**Barley Tea**- May be used for aiding digestion and promoting weight loss.

**Dandelion Tea** - May be helpful in aiding digestion and promoting weight loss.

**Cranberry Tea** - May be helpful in treating some bacterial infections, mostly in urinary tract infections in both infants, children, and adults.

**Thyme Tea** - May help with problems related to respiratory, nervous, and cardiovascular systems.

**Nettle Tea** - May help reduce the risk of heart diseases, cancer, and diabetes, and has a positive effect on blood pressure, and even psychotic disorders.

# Disclaimer

I am not a licensed practitioner, therefore the descriptions regarding the benefits and safety of the herbal teas listed above have not been evaluated by the Food and Drug administration. They are not intended to diagnose, prevent, treat, or cure any disease. This information does not constitute medical advice and it should not be relied upon as such. Consult with your doctor before modifying your medical regime.

# Day1

**Chamomile Tea**

Psalm 24:1 "The earth is the LORD's and the fulness thereof; the world, and they that dwell therein."

We must understand everything belongs to God, whether it's the people we talk to, the ground we walk on, or the trees and lilies of the field - it all belongs to God.

**What did God speak to me:**

_____

_____

_____

_____

_____

_____

_____

_____

# Day 2

### Peppermint Tea

Jeremiah 29:11 "For I know the thoughts that I think toward you, saith the LORD, thoughts of peace, and not of evil, to give you an expected end."

No matter what is going on in your life right now, know that God's intentions toward you are good and working together for a greater purpose.

### What did God speak to me:

_____

_____

_____

_____

_____

_____

_____

# Day 3

## Ginger Tea

John 4:24 "God is a spirit: and they that worship him must worship him in spirit and in truth."

Our spirit longs to worship God, the creator. We must posture ourselves before an almighty God to accept His truth concerning us.

## What did God speak to me:

_____

_____

_____

_____

_____

_____

_____

# Day 4

## Nettle Tea

Psalm 37:1-2 "Fret not thyself because of evildoers, neither be thou envious against the workers of iniquity. For they shall soon be cut down like the grass and wither as the green herb."

**The enemy you see today, you will not see tomorrow.**

**What did God speak to me:**

_____

_____

_____

_____

_____

_____

_____

_____

# Day 5

**Lemongrass Tea**

John 11:35 "Jesus Wept." Understand that God sees your tears and has not forgotten about you.

It's ok to cry for a moment but know that God has got this one! Look up!!

**What did God speak to me:**

_____

_____

_____

_____

_____

_____

_____

_____

# Day 6

### Jasmine Tea

Hebrews 11:6 "But without faith it is impossible to please him: for he that cometh to God must believe that he is, and that he is a rewarder of them that diligently seek him."

God wants us to trust Him for everything. He is our creator and has great plans for us. We must not doubt God's ability to make good on His promises. Do not doubt, but believe it in your heart and you will soon see the manifestation of the rewards from your diligence.

### What did God speak to me:

_____

_____

_____

_____

_____

_____

# Day 7

## Rose Hip Tea

1 Corinthians 2:9 "But as it is written, Eye hath not seen, nor ear heard, neither have entered into the heart of man, the things which God hath prepared for them that love him."

You are on the cusp of a major breakthrough in your life. So, what if the world doesn't see it in you - God is setting you up for something great!

## What did God speak to me:

_____

_____

_____

_____

_____

_____

_____

_____

# Day 8

## Cinnamon Tea

Psalm 50:10 "For every beast of the forest is mine, and the cattle upon a thousand hills."

Whatever you need from God today, because you are His, you have been granted access. Just ask!

## What did God speak to me:

_____

_____

_____

_____

_____

_____

_____

_____

# Day 9

### Olive Leaf Tea

1 Corinthians 13:13 "And now abideth faith, hope, charity, these three; but the greatest of these is charity."

Have you checked your love walk lately? Do you love people as Christ Loves us? Though it's good to have faith and hope in God, we must possess the agape type of Love that God has and allow it to show forth toward His people.

## What did God speak to me:

_____

_____

_____

_____

_____

_____

_____

_____

# Day 10

## Elderberry Tea

Psalm 19:14 "Let the words of my mouth, and the meditation of my heart, be acceptable in thy sight, O LORD, my strength, and my redeemer."

Every day seek to please the Lord in all that you do. When faced with challenging situations and things that may make you angry or want to respond in an ungodly manner, ask yourself this question: "What would Jesus do?" This will help us to exemplify Christ and allow Him to be our help.

## What did God speak to me:

_____

_____

_____

_____

_____

_____

# Day 11

## Barley Tea

Philippians 4:13 "I can do all things through Christ which strengtheneth me."

No matter what we face in life or what we find ourselves going through, we know that we can make it with the strength of our Lord working through us.

## What did God speak to me:

_____

_____

_____

_____

_____

_____

_____

_____

_____

# Day 12

### Thyme Tea

Psalm 28:7 "The LORD is my strength and my shield; my heart trusted in him, and I am helped: therefore, my heart greatly rejoiceth; and with my song will I praise him."

Every day presents us with some type of opposition. Whether it's about our job, at home, our children, finances, etc., but we must recognize that the Lord will continue to see us through.

### What did God speak to me:

_____

_____

_____

_____

_____

_____

_____

# Day 13

### Ashwagandha Tea

Proverbs 14:30 "A sound heart is the life of the flesh: but envy the rottenness of the bones."

It is important to make peace and be at peace with all men, as our bodies take a toll on us because of what we hold inside. Release those that hurt you, disappoint you, abandon you, blame you, embarrass you, and forgive them and let it go! Here you will find an inner peace causing you to love and soar beyond while fueling your body for change.

### What did God speak to me:

_____

_____

_____

_____

_____

_____

# Day 14

### Rooibos Tea

Ecclesiastes 3:11 "He hath made everything beautiful in his time: also, he hath set the world in their heart, so that no man can find out the work that God maketh from the beginning to the end."

You are a diamond in the rough right now. God is shaping and molding you into the woman of God He created you to be. You may not like how you are right now, but God is not through with you yet. You are just about ready to be presented to the body to fulfill your God-given purpose.

### What did God speak to me:

_____

_____

_____

_____

_____

_____

_____

_____

# Day 15

## Cranberry Tea

Jude 1:2 "Mercy unto you, and peace, and love, be multiplied."

Today, thank God for His mercy, peace, and love that he gives us on a daily basis. There are so many things God showed us mercy in. So many times, we could have lost our minds but He gave us peace, and He showed us His love through the loving people He has surrounded us with. What a mighty God we serve.

## What did God speak to me:

_____

_____

_____

_____

_____

_____

_____

_____

# Day 16

## Eucalyptus Tea

Job 37:14 "Hearken unto this, O Job: stand still and consider the wondrous works of God."

Before you complain today, stop and think of God's goodness with purpose. Think about all the wonderful things He has done and is doing in your life. Give God praise for this present situation and see Him in it - and know that it's working for your good.

## What did God speak to me:

_____

_____

_____

_____

_____

_____

# Day 17

### Raspberry Tea

Psalm 138:8 "The Lord will perfect that which concerneth me: thy mercy, O LORD, endureth forever: forsake not the works of thine own hands."

The Lord will fulfill His purpose for me. Know this, the Lord has not forgotten about you. For the promises of God are yet 'yes and amen' in your life. You will see the manifestation of His glory in your life.

### What did God speak to me:

_____

_____

_____

_____

_____

_____

_____

_____

# Day 18

### Dandelion Tea

Psalm 126:3 "The LORD hath done great things for us; whereof we are glad."

Be thankful for all that God has done for you, as it could be worse. Have you ever thought that you were the only one going through something, but then God showed you someone else and your spirit ignited with joy knowing that your situation is not as bad as you thought?

### What did God speak to me:

_____

_____

_____

_____

_____

_____

_____

# Day 19

## Chamomile Tea

Matthew 5:16 "Let your light so shine before men, that they may see your good works, and glorify your Father which is in heaven."

No matter what you face today, let your light shine before men. We don't have to always show what we're going through or how we feel but let the light of God show through you that His Glory might be revealed.

## What did God speak to me:

_____

_____

_____

_____

_____

_____

_____

_____

# Day 20

### Peppermint Tea

James 1:17 "Every good gift and every perfect gift is from above, and cometh down from the Father of lights, with whom is no variableness, neither shadow of turning.

Many of us have been gifted to do many things, whether it's hospitality, to give words of encouragement, to do hair, to work with children, to prophesy, or whatever it may be. We must know that it came from God.

### What did God speak to me:

_____

_____

_____

_____

_____

_____

_____

_____

# Day 21

## Rosehip Tea

Philippians 4:4 "Rejoice in the Lord always: and again, I say, Rejoice."

Many of us, as believers in the Lord, know to rejoice in the Lord. However, when situations come, we may find it difficult to do so, as we don't understand why God would allow it to be happening. The latter part of scripture says - and again I say - rejoice. So, after we have known to rejoice - giving the excuse of why we cannot, don't feel like it - God says to rejoice. So, rejoice anyhow, it's going to get better. This is not the end for you.

## What did God speak to me:

_____

_____

_____

_____

_____

_____

# Day 22

**Rooibos Tea**

Proverbs 17:17 "A friend loveth at all times, and a brother is born for adversity."

What type of friend are you? Do you drop friends when they are going through something, or they don't do what you advise them to do, or even if their lifestyle isn't as becoming as yours? Imagine your own life if, when you needed a friend, no-one was there. Stop dropping people - you never know who you'll need later.

**What did God speak to me:**

_____

_____

_____

_____

_____

_____

_____

_____

# Day 23

## Ginger Tea

1 John 4:19 "We love him, because he first loved us."

Our love for others should be like that of the Father, as He loves us unconditionally. But for many of us, we love based on conditions. If you do this then I love you, if you have this then I love you, if you love me then I love you. These are some of the ways some people extend love, but this is not God's love. He loves us when we don't do what He requires, He loves us when we have or don't have anything, He even loves us when we don't love Him back. Today, exemplify the love of God towards others - you can do it.

## What did God speak to me:

_____

_____

_____

_____

_____

_____

_____

# Day 24

## Cinnamon Tea

Romans 15:13 "Now the God of hope fill you with all joy and peace in believing, that ye may abound in hope, through the power of the Holy Ghost."

Look to the Lord today and trust Him totally with your family, finances, health, and wellbeing etc., as He knows what you are up against. There is hope! Our God will not allow you to lose, so take His joy, take His peace, and live!

## What did God speak to me:

_____

_____

_____

_____

_____

_____

# Day 25

## Lemongrass Tea

Luke 10:19 "Behold, I give unto you power to tread on serpents and scorpions, and over all the power of the enemy: and nothing shall by any means hurt you."

You have been given authority over your present situations. Begin to speak and declare to the atmosphere the change you seek. There is no need to fear as Jesus is near! He's got your back. Decree it!

## What did God speak to me:

_____

_____

_____

_____

_____

_____

_____

_____

# Day 26

### Olive Leaf Tea

2 Kings 7:3 "And there were four leprous men at the entering in of the gate: and they said one to another, Why sit we here until we die?"

Today it's up to you to decide whether to live or die. Will you allow your circumstances to hinder you from moving forward in God or will you RISE UP AND WIN?

### What did God speak to me:

_____

_____

_____

_____

_____

_____

# Day 27

## Eucalyptus Tea

Isaiah 57:1 "The righteous perisheth, and no man layeth it to heart: and merciful men are taken away, none considering that the righteous is taken away from the evil to come."

As believers, we never really know the evil and dangers God protects us from. So, when life throws a curveball, just lift your hands and give Him praise that you are still here.

## What did God speak to me:

_____

_____

_____

_____

_____

_____

_____

_____

# Day 28

## Ashwagandha Tea

Hosea 12:6 "Therefore turn thou to thy God: keep mercy and judgment, and wait on thy God continually."

We must know that our strength lies totally in God. Though we do not understand fully what's going on, we must wait continually.

## What did God speak to me:

_____

_____

_____

_____

_____

_____

_____

_____

# Day 29

## Raspberry Tea

Daniel 12:12 "Blessed is he that waiteth, and cometh to the thousand three hundred and five and thirty days."

This is a long time to wait. However, no matter what God has promised you, don't give up but wait until the change comes. You will be blessed for enduring until the end.

## What did God speak to me:

_____

_____

_____

_____

_____

_____

_____

_____

# Day 30

## Elderberry Tea

Numbers 30:2 "If a man vow a vow unto the LORD or swear an oath to bind his soul with a bond; he shall not break his word, he shall do according to all that proceedeth out of his mouth."

Vows are very important and are meant to be kept. If you find it difficult to keep your vow, talk to whomever you made the vow with; don't ignore them or hope they forget what you said. Talk, be honest, and make good on what you said.

### What did God speak to me:

_____

_____

_____

_____

_____

_____

# Day 31

## Chamomile Tea

Esther 5:6 "And the King said unto Esther at the banquet of wine, what is thy petition? and it shall be granted thee; and what is thy request? even to the half of the kingdom it shall be performed."

As we position ourselves in the presence of the King, the Almighty one, He is more than willing to hear our petitions and requests and grant them to us. Do you not know that you are favored by God? If God is not granting your petitions and your requests, why not?

## What did God speak to me:

_____

_____

_____

_____

_____

_____

_____

_____

# Day 32

## Moringa Tea

John 15:12 "This is my commandment, that ye love one another, as I have loved you."

It would be amazing if we all would love as Christ loved us. Many times, we allow circumstances, people who may have wronged us, lied to us, left us, or don't agree with us to shape how we choose to love. If God loves us unconditionally and we are created in His image, why is it hard for you to show genuine love?

## What did God speak to me:

_____

_____

_____

_____

_____

_____

_____

_____

# Day 33

## Jasmine Tea

Proverbs 11:24-25 "One person gives freely, yet gains even more; another withholds unduly, but comes to poverty. A generous person will prosper; whoever refreshes others will be refreshed. (NIV)"

Everything that we have and have been given belongs to the Lord. Whatever He desires from me, I say yes, knowing that if He has need of it, then He is more than able to replenish it. If you give freely to others not expecting anything back from them, your return from God will be greater than that which you gave.

## What did God speak to me:

_____

_____

_____

_____

_____

_____

# Day 34

## Barley Tea

Isaiah 41:10: "Fear thou not; for I am with thee: be not dismayed; for I am thy God: I will strengthen thee; yea, I will help thee; yea, I will uphold thee with the right hand of my righteousness."

There are times that we feel we are alone in our present situations and it is important to know that God is very near, though we can't feel Him or trace Him. God is always there to strengthen us and help us through. You are not alone! God can and will see you through. Pick your head up, you are just about to break on through to the other side!!

## What did God speak to me:

_____

_____

_____

_____

_____

_____

# Day 35

## Dandelion Tea

Romans 9:22 "What if God, willing to shew his wrath, and to make his power known, endured with much longsuffering the vessels of wrath fitted to destruction:"

How many of us can honestly say that we would willingly suffer for an extended period of time for someone else's greater good (easier said than done)? Perhaps for our immediate family we may do so, but what about for someone you may not even know?

## What did God speak to me:

_____

_____

_____

_____

_____

_____

_____

# Day 36

### Cranberry Tea

Deuteronomy 8:18 But thou shalt remember the LORD thy God: for it is he that giveth thee power to get wealth, that he may establish his covenant which he sware unto thy fathers, as it is this day."

God desires for you to live a wealthy and prosperous life. You being poor is not His will for your life. What idea has God given you, what dream or vision do you have that you've been sitting on? The ideas and thoughts are not yours, they are God's. Move forward!!

### What did God speak to me:

_____

_____

_____

_____

_____

_____

# Day 37

### Thyme Tea

Exodus 14:13-14" And Moses said unto the people, Fear ye not, stand still, and see the salvation of the LORD, which he will shew to you today: for the Egyptians whom ye have seen today, ye shall see them again no more forever.

The LORD shall fight for you, and ye shall hold your peace." Whatever you are facing right now, all you have to do is put it in God's hands and know that he will fight for you. No need to worry or try to see your way out of it. GOD'S GOT YOUR BACK!

### What did God speak to me:

_____

_____

_____

_____

_____

_____

# Day 38

## Nettle Tea

Colossians 3:5 "Mortify therefore your members which are upon the earth; fornication, uncleanness, inordinate affection, evil concupiscence, and covetousness, which is idolatry:"

Daily we must strive to walk in the spirit, putting away sin which is not pleasing to God. If we are struggling in an area, seek God's help and Godly counsel so that you do not fall into a lifestyle of sin. We each have a choice. Which will you choose?

### What did God speak to me:

_____

_____

_____

_____

_____

_____

_____

_____

# Day 39

## Chamomile Tea

I Corinthians 13: 4-5 "Charity suffereth long, and is kind; charity envieth not; charity vaunteth not itself, is not puffed up, Doth not behave itself unseemly, seeketh not her own, is not easily provoked, thinketh no evil;"

When you truly love someone, there is no room to be jealous or envious of anyone. You truly want to see them prosper. Genuine love is heartfelt and isn't forced. It comes from the heart. Do you truly love those around you? Do they feel it's genuine?

## What did God speak to me:

_____

_____

_____

_____

_____

_____

# Day 40

### Peppermint Tea

Matthew 5:9 "Blessed are the peacemakers: for they shall be called the children of God."

Are you one who seeks to bring peace in a situation or one who brings the confusion? Seek peace with all men. Don't be the one who brings and carries the latest gossip.

### What did God speak to me:

_____

_____

_____

_____

_____

_____

_____

_____

# Day 41

## RoseHip Tea

Exodus 20:12 "Honour thy father and thy mother: that thy days may be long upon the land which the LORD thy God giveth thee."

Honoring parents that have abused us, abandoned us, wronged us, etc. in many cases is very hard to do as we feel that they aren't worthy of our honour. After all, parents should do the right thing concerning their children. Well, they don't always. Yet we still have to show them honor if we intend to honor God and His word. We must do what is right in the sight of God and we will receive our just reward from Him as a result of our obedience.

## What did God speak to me:

_____

_____

_____

_____

_____

# Day 42

### Rooibos Tea

I Corinthians 6:5 "I speak to your shame. Is it so, that there is not a wise man among you? No, not one that shall be able to judge between his brethren?"

Oftentimes, we are ashamed of our behavior or past faults, and the guilt of them will not let us go. We have those around us who constantly remind us of it and treat us as if we will never change. Listen, despite your shame, you must know that all of us have something we are ashamed about. Whatever you do not allow the voices around you to keep you in a place of shame. There is NO ONE that can judge. Let it Go!! You have been forgiven. Now walk therein…

### What did God speak to me:

_____

_____

_____

_____

# Day 43

### Ginger Tea

Jeremiah 17:14 "Heal me, O LORD, and I shall be healed; save me, and I shall be saved: for thou art my praise."

Whatever your ailment is today, just ask of the Lord to heal and you shall be healed. Begin to give Him praise and thank Him for your healing. Begin decreeing and commanding your body to line up and it will obey!

### What did God speak to me:

_____

_____

_____

_____

_____

_____

_____

_____

# Day 44

### Cinnamon Tea

Mark 11:25 "And when ye stand praying, forgive, if ye have ought against any: that your Father also which is in heaven may forgive you your trespasses."

Why is it that we as a people seek God's forgiveness but we will not forgive our brethren? God quickly forgives us and yet we have a hard time. It's time for you to do a heart check. You can't get what you aren't first willing to give of yourself.

### What did God speak to me:

_____

_____

_____

_____

_____

_____

_____

_____

# Day 45

## Jasmine Tea

Romans 12:12 "Rejoicing in hope; patient in tribulation; continuing instant in prayer;"

The Lord is intervening on your behalf right now. You have patiently endured this situation and the Lord is setting you up! It's been a long time coming but your setback is making room for your comeback.

## What did God speak to me:

_____

_____

_____

_____

_____

_____

# Day 46

### Lemongrass Tea

1 John 2:29 "If ye know that he is righteous, ye know that everyone that doeth righteousness is born of him."

Every day is an opportunity to walk in the righteousness of God. We do not get to have an off day because He is righteous - and so are we if we are born of Him.

### What did God speak to me:

_____

_____

_____

_____

_____

_____

_____

# Day 47

### Olive Leaf Tea

Matthew 21:22 - "And all things, whatsoever ye shall ask in prayer, believing, ye shall receive."

What is it that you are asking God for? A home, business, finances, healing, etc.

Check this out…You shall see it when you believe it! See yourself walking in your healing, see yourself driving that brand new car, see yourself moving into your dream home, see yourself with the promotion, SEE YOURSELF THERE and watch - not too many days hence you will be right where you want to be.

### What did God speak to me:

_____

_____

_____

_____

_____

# Day 48

### Eucalyptus Tea

2 Corinthians 9:7 "Every man according as he purposeth in his heart, so let him give; not grudgingly, or of necessity: for God loveth a cheerful giver."

I know we heard this scripture a lot in Church as it relates to money, but I can't tell you how this scripture bears witness with me and all that I do. I realize that what I have doesn't belong to me and if God gave it to me and desires for me to give, I shouldn't do it grudgingly. Why? Because He is God the giver of all things and I as His daughter shall never be without.

### What did God speak to me:

_____

_____

_____

_____

_____

# Day 49

## Rosehip Tea

Philippians 4:6 "Be careful about nothing; but in everything by prayer and supplication with thanksgiving let your requests be made known unto God."

If something, has you worrying today, pray about it and make your request known to God. He is the only one who can turn this around to work in your favor. Say this with me:" I will not be overtaken."

## What did God speak to me:

_____

_____

_____

_____

_____

_____

_____

_____

# Day 50

## Ashwagandha Tea

Amos 8:11 "Behold, the days come, saith the Lord GOD, that I will send a famine in the land, not a famine of bread, nor a thirst for water, but of hearing the words of the LORD:"

During this time of spiritual famine, the prophets, preachers, and teachers were scarce. I want to submit to you today to hear God's word, read God's word and hide it in your heart. When you can't hear the preacher today or have your bible handy and you are faced with a situation, you can pull His word from your heart arsenal as the word lives in you.

## What did God speak to me:

_____

_____

_____

_____

_____

# Day 51

### Raspberry Tea

1 John 4:1 "Beloved, believe not every spirit, but try the spirits whether they are of God: because many false prophets are gone out into the world."

It is important that you are able to discern what spirit is speaking to you. Don't get so caught up in the way people speak and how gifted they seem. For there is a thin line between the prophet, the psychic, the witch, and the warlock. Know the difference.

### What did God speak to me:

_____

_____

_____

_____

_____

_____

# Day 52

**Elderberry Tea**

Romans 10:17 "So then faith cometh by hearing, and hearing by the word of God."

There are many truths in the word of God and, as we hear what the spirit is saying unto us, we develop the faith to know that he is not a God that should lie. Keep the faith and keep it moving, and as you do so you will begin to see the manifestation thereof.

**What did God speak to me:**

_____

_____

_____

_____

_____

_____

_____

# Day 53

## Jasmine Tea

James 1:2 "My brethren, count it all joy when ye fall into divers temptations;"

This is not the time to be defeated; but the bible says to consider it all joy! Know that you will not stay here but you will get up! So, rejoice in the Lord always.

## What did God speak to me:

_____

_____

_____

_____

_____

_____

_____

_____

# Day 54

**Barley Tea**

Philippians 4:13 "I can do all things through Christ which strengtheneth me."

There is not anything you can't do when you have the strength of Christ at your side. Just look around you at all that is in the world that you have access to every day. Someone had the courage to build and design the car you drive, the bed you sleep in, the books you read, the place you work, etc. Do you think there were days that they needed the strength of the Lord when they were mocked for their vision which may have seemed silly? Heck yeah! What is it that you want to do?? Why aren't you doing it, and doing it BIG??

**What did God speak to me:**

_____

_____

_____

_____

_____

# Day 55

## Dandelion Tea

Psalms 5:12 "For thou, LORD, wilt bless the righteous; with favour wilt thou compass him as with a shield."

When you have been favored by God, there isn't anything that anyone can do or say to remove it. As the old cliche goes, Favour ain't fair. Walk in your favor, for there are limitless opportunities for you - all you have to do is walk through the door. Favor is already there.

## What did God speak to me:

_____

_____

_____

_____

_____

_____

# Day 56

## Cranberry Tea

Matthew 6:26 "Behold the fowls of the air: for they sow not, neither do they reap, nor gather into barns; yet your heavenly Father feedeth them. Are ye not much better than they?"

God is saying that you are worthy to receive. Believe that! You are significant and a partaker of His many blessings.

## What did God speak to me:

_____

_____

_____

_____

_____

_____

# Day 57

## Thyme Tea

Isaiah 1:19-20 "If ye be willing and obedient, ye shall eat the good of the land: But if ye refuse and rebel, ye shall be devoured with the sword: for the mouth of the LORD hath spoken it."

When you are both willing and obedient, you can eat the good of the land. It is imperative that you are not just obedient but also willing. There are things at times that we do because we know it's the right thing to do, but our hearts are far from it and we wish we didn't have to do it.

Could this be why you aren't experiencing the fullness of God's blessings for you? You are obedient but you do not have a willing heart. Heart check.

Ex. As a child, were you ever forced to make up with your brother or sister and tell them you're sorry? You did it but you sure didn't want to! You may have kicked and screamed or left with your mouth pouting. There is a reason God said WILLING & OBEDIENT.

## What did God speak to me:

_____

_____

# Day 58

## Nettle Tea

Romans 15:13 "Now the God of hope fill you with all joy and peace in believing, that ye may abound in hope, through the power of the Holy Ghost."

Here we see that we need the power of the Holy Ghost to continue on in our hope. There are days that we want to throw in the towel, but through the power of the Holy Ghost we are able to continue on knowing that our hope will soon be fulfilled.

## What did God speak to me:

_____

_____

_____

_____

_____

_____

# Day 59

## Moringa Tea

Acts 2:17 "And it shall come to pass in the last days, saith God, I will pour out of my Spirit upon all flesh: and your sons and your daughters shall prophesy, and your young men shall see visions, and your old men shall dream dreams:"

We are now living in a time where God has poured out His spirit to us to tap into the spiritual realm where God is and to tap into what He is doing within the Earth. Where are you in the midst?

### What did God speak to me:

_____

_____

_____

_____

_____

_____

_____

_____

_____

# Day 60

## Chamomile Tea

Ephesians 3:16-17 "That he would grant you, according to the riches of his glory, to be strengthened with might by his Spirit in the inner man; That Christ may dwell in your hearts by faith; that ye, being rooted and grounded in love,"

It is through Faith in God that we are able to experience that inner peace and strength knowing that God loves us and cares for us.

## What did God speak to me:

_____

_____

_____

_____

_____

_____

# Day 61

## Peppermint Tea

Colossians 3:14 "And over all these virtues put on love, which binds them all together in perfect unity."

When we operate in a spirit of Love in all that we do, we can easily bring our families, communities, and even our nation together.

## What did God speak to me:

_____

_____

_____

_____

_____

_____

_____

_____

# Day 62

### RoseHip Tea

Acts 20:35 "I have shewed you all things, how that so labouring ye ought to support the weak, and to remember the words of the Lord Jesus, how he said, It is more blessed to give than to receive."

Don't be one who always has their hand out for a handout, but always be found giving to others whenever and wherever you can even with the little you may have.

### What did God speak to me:

_____

_____

_____

_____

_____

_____

# Day 63

## Roobios Tea

Nehemiah 8:10 "Do not grieve, for the joy of the Lord is your strength."

Oftentimes, our trials in life cause us to grieve. While this is normal for us, we must always remember that God is near and able to give us the strength to continue on, despite what we may be feeling right now.

## What did God speak to me:

_____

_____

_____

_____

_____

_____

# Day 64

### Ginger Tea

John 16:33 "These things I have spoken unto you, that in me ye might have peace. In the world ye shall have tribulation: but be of good cheer; I have overcome the world."

Wherever you are in life right now, understand that it's not the end of the world for you. Look at your situation from a different perspective and receive the peace of God knowing that you too can overcome.

### What did God speak to me:

_____

_____

_____

_____

_____

_____

# Day 65

## Cinnamon Tea

Ephesians 4:32 "And be ye kind one to another, tenderhearted, forgiving one another, even as God for Christ's sake hath forgiven you."

It is important that we operate with the same forgiveness as our heavenly father. We can't expect to have God's forgiveness and yet still hold grudges against others. We have to forgive, though it may hurt, so that we are in right standing with God.

## What did God speak to me:

_____

_____

_____

_____

_____

_____

# Day 66

**Lemongrass Tea**

Psalm 147:3 "He healeth the broken in heart, and bindeth up their wounds."

Whatever you have experienced in life, whether it's a bad relationship, loss of a loved one, job loss, etc., God is able to heal and mend your broken heart. Turn it over to the Lord.

**What did God speak to me:**

_____

_____

_____

_____

_____

_____

_____

# Day 67

### Olive Leaf Tea

1 Thessalonians 5:16-18 "Rejoice evermore. Pray without ceasing. In everything give thanks: for this is the will of God in Christ Jesus concerning you."

I know sometimes when life throws us a curveball it can be difficult to give God thanks or praise in the midst of it. However, God desires for us to give Him thanks for everything and in everything. Whether things are good or whether you feel they are not, it is His will that we do so.

### What did God speak to me:

_____

_____

_____

_____

# Day 68

**Eucalyptus Tea**

Luke 8:50 "But when Jesus heard it, he answered him, saying, Fear not: believe only, and she shall be made whole."

When God speaks, we need to hearken unto His voice no matter how silly it looks or how impossible it may seem. If He said it then IT IS SO!! Believe it!

**What did God speak to me:**

_____

_____

_____

_____

_____

_____

_____

# Day 69

### Ashwagandha Tea

Numbers 6:24-26 "The LORD bless thee, and keep thee: The LORD make his face shine upon thee, and be gracious unto thee: The LORD lift up his countenance upon thee, and give thee peace."

As you go about your daily routine, understand that God is with you and God is for you. Allow the peace of God to keep with you as you work, deal with your children, your business, and any life affairs that you have going on. You are covered!

### What did God speak to me:

_____

_____

_____

_____

_____

_____

# Day 70

**Raspberry Tea** 1 Corinthians 13:4-5 "Charity suffereth long, and is kind; charity envieth not; charity vaunteth not itself, is not puffed up, Doth not behave itself unseemly, seeketh not her own, is not easily provoked, thinketh no evil."

When you truly love someone, there isn't anything that you wouldn't do for them, and this love is shown by you and felt by the recipient. It is important for us to adopt this type of love not only with our immediate family but also with others who can seem so hard to love.

### What did God speak to me:

_____

_____

_____

_____

_____

# Day 71

## Elderberry Tea

Matthew 25:21 "His lord said unto him. Well done, thou good and faithful servant: thou hast been faithful over a few things, I will make thee ruler over many things: enter thou into the joy of thy lord."

Never complain about the little that you have, but instead be joyous knowing that God desires to give you more. Can God trust you with what you have now? Are you doing what you are supposed to be doing right now with the little that you have?

## What did God speak to me:

_____

_____

_____

_____

_____

_____

# Day 72

### Jasmine Tea

Mark 11:24 "Therefore I say unto you, what things soever ye desire, when ye pray, believe that ye receive them, and then ye shall have them."

It is important that when we pray, we don't pray amiss. We must believe that we can have what we ask for according to His will. Now, that does not mean that you can ask Him for someone else's spouse, but rather that you believe your spouse is tailor-made for you.

### What did God speak to me:

_____

_____

_____

_____

_____

_____

# Day 73

## Barley Tea

Matthew 6:14 "For if ye forgive men their trespasses, your heavenly Father will also forgive you:"

We have to know that forgiving others is a prerequisite to our own forgiveness. We cannot walk around holding grudges against people who may have harmed us physically, mentally, or verbally. Our Lord and Savior Jesus Christ was crucified for us and yet forgave the one who crucified Him.

## What did God speak to me:

_____

_____

_____

_____

_____

_____

_____

_____

# Day 74

## Dandelion Tea

John 14:23 "Jesus answered and said unto him, If a man love me, he will keep my words: and my Father will love him, and we will come unto him, and make our abode with him."

When we truly love the Lord Jesus, it is shown in our actions when keeping His word. Our daily actions should resemble that of the Lord if we are actively keeping the word of God hidden in our hearts. As we keep His word, God will rest within us.

## What did God speak to me:

_____

_____

_____

_____

_____

_____

_____

_____

# Day 75

## Cranberry Tea

Romans 12:19 "Dearly beloved, avenge not yourselves, but rather give place unto wrath:for it is written, Vengeance is mine; I will repay, saith the Lord."

Whatever wrong has been done against or towards us, we are not to fight our own battles. We must step aside and place that in the Lord's hands as He will fight on our behalf.

## What did God speak to me:

_____

_____

_____

_____

_____

_____

_____

_____

# Day 76

## Thyme Tea

Psalm 86:15 "But thou, O lord, art a God full of compassion, and gracious, longsuffering, and plenteous in mercy and truth."

Do you have the ability to see past where one is right now and see them how God sees them? We must remember that we were not always where we are today, and we must extend that same loving compassion and grace towards others.

## What did God speak to me:

_____

_____

_____

_____

_____

_____

_____

# Day 77

### Nettle Tea

Ephesians 4:26-27 "Be ye angry, and sin not: let not the sun go down upon your wrath: Neither give place to the devil."

In our relationships with our spouses, children, family, friends, co-workers, etc., it is important that we seek to make things right the same day. Do not allow things to carry over to the next day, week, month, or over year and years. When we do this, we sin against God's word because we have allowed sin to enter by walking in anger and unforgiveness.

### What did God speak to me:

_____

_____

_____

_____

_____

_____

# Day 78

## Moringa Tea

Luke 8:50 "But when Jesus heard it, he answered him, saying, Fear not: believe only, and she shall be made whole."

We see here God's ability to make a dead girl rise again. So, I say to you that no matter what it looks like, if you will believe and do not allow fear to overtake you, God can and will make you whole again.

## What did God speak to me:

_____

_____

_____

_____

_____

_____

_____

# Day 79

### Chamomile Tea

1John 4:16 "And so we know and rely on the love God has for us. God is love. Whoever lives in love lives in God, and God in them."

If we say or profess that we love God, then we should also Love what and who God loves. Love should be exemplified in our talk and our walk so that it may be seen and felt by those around us wherever we go.

### What did God speak to me:

_____

_____

_____

_____

_____

_____

_____

_____

# Day 80

### Peppermint Tea

1 Samuel 15:23 "For rebellion is as the sin of witchcraft, and stubbornness is as iniquity and idolatry. Because thou hast rejected the word of the LORD, he hath also rejected thee from being king."

The word of God gives us instructions on how to live our daily lives and is full of examples pertaining to everyday living and real-life situations. We must strive every day to adhere to the principles of God so that we might live a fruitful and peaceful life.

### What did God speak to me:

_____

_____

_____

_____

_____

_____

# Day 81

## RoseHip Tea

Hebrews 11:1 "Now faith is the substance of things hoped for, the evidence of things not seen."

There are many things that God has promised us that we have not yet seen come to pass in our lives. However, we must continue to trust that God will do just as He promised because our faith lives in Him.

## What did God speak to me:

_____

_____

_____

_____

_____

_____

_____

_____

# Day 82

### Ginger Tea

Proverbs 10:22 "The blessing of the LORD, it maketh rich, and he addeth no sorrow with it."

Riches obtained the right way through the leading of the Lord will leave you with a spirit of joy. You are blessed to give to others as the Lord increases you. However, if you are not able to enjoy what you have, check where the riches came from and the manner in which you obtained them. All money isn't good money.

### What did God speak to me:

_____

_____

_____

_____

_____

_____

# Day 83

## Cinnamon Tea

Psalm 118:24 "This is the day which the LORD hath made; we will rejoice and be glad in it."

Every day is a gift from the Lord, and we should ever be so grateful that we were able to wake up! Despite what is happening around us, it is still a good time to rejoice knowing that our God is our protector, peace, and comfort.

## What did God speak to me:

_____

_____

_____

_____

_____

_____

_____

_____

# Day 84

### Lemongrass Tea

1 Corinthians 15:58 "Therefore, my beloved brethren, be ye stedfast, unmoveable, always abounding in the work of the Lord, forasmuch as ye know that your labour is not in vain in the Lord."

God's timing is impeccable! So always be found pushing forward no matter what it looks like with a surety that God will surely show up on your behalf. As the old folks would say, "He may not come when you want Him, but He'll be there right on time". God has not forgotten about you.

### What did God speak to me:

_____

_____

_____

_____

_____

_____

# Day 85

## Raspberry Tea

Luke 6:37 "Judge not, and ye shall not be judged: condemn not, and ye shall not be condemned: forgive, and ye shall be forgiven:"

It is important that we walk in the same way our God does as it relates to His people. We all have sinned against God and done wrong to others. Therefore, we must humble ourselves and extend the same grace towards others that our loving and faithful God shows towards us.

## What did God speak to me:

_____

_____

_____

_____

_____

_____

_____

_____

# Day 86

### Dandelion Tea

John 14:27 "Peace I leave with you, my peace I give unto you: not as the world giveth, give I unto you. Let not your heart be troubled, neither let it be afraid."

As we go about in our daily lives, having God's peace over us and in us helps to keep us sound and grounded knowing that He is near so there's no need to fear.

### What did God speak to me:

_____

_____

_____

_____

_____

_____

_____

# Day 87

## Cranberry Tea

Numbers 14:18 "The LORD is longsuffering, and of great mercy, forgiving iniquity and transgression, and by no means clearing the guilty, visiting the iniquity of the fathers upon the children unto the third and fourth generation."

We see here how faithful God is to us when we mess up and yet He continues to show forth His mercy towards us. However, he also tells us that by no means are our actions okay and He being God allows the iniquity of our bad choices to be visited upon our children. Ever wondered why you see yourself in your children or see in them Uncle June Bug or Aunt Sally? Though God is faithful, our actions and deeds still matter.

## What did God speak to me:

_____

_____

_____

_____

_____

_____

# Day 88

**Thyme Tea**

Proverbs 13:11 "Wealth gotten by vanity shall be diminished: but he that gathereth by labour shall increase."

We have to be ever so careful that we are not drawn away by get-rich-quick schemes and doing things that are not pleasing in the sight of God to accumulate wealth. We do not cheat to get ahead or step on others to succeed as this never lasts. But when you work for your wealth and apply the principles of God, you will see a major improvement in your life.

**What did God speak to me:**

_____

_____

_____

_____

_____

_____

# Day 89

### Moringa Tea

1Corinthians 16:14 "Do everything in love."

When you do things for people make sure to check your motives and the spirit behind what you do. Are you doing it because you genuinely love the person or because you're being made to do something you really don't want to do? When you do things because you're being made to, that Love isn't always felt as genuine. Develop a true Love for God's people that one can freely receive.

### What did God speak to me:

_____

_____

_____

_____

_____

_____

# Day 90

## Jasmine Tea

James 1:3 "Knowing this, that the trying of your faith worketh patience."

As we are believing God and standing in faith, it definitely shows us how to be patient. We as a people want things expeditiously, as we want to rush the process - such as when you microwave food because you can't wait for it to heat up on the stove or in the oven. Some things you need to wait on. A delay does not mean a denial. WAIT!

## What did God speak to me:

_____

_____

_____

_____

_____

_____

# NOTES

Morning Tea with THE KING

Daily Devotional

TISH BARNHARDT

Made in the USA
Middletown, DE
04 June 2021